THE WORLD OF STEM

The STEM of Airplanes

By Fiona Young-Brown

Cavendish Square
New York

Published in 2021 by Cavendish Square Publishing, LLC
243 5th Avenue, Suite 136, New York, NY 10016

First Edition

Website: cavendishsq.com

Cataloging-in-Publication Data

Names: Young-Brown, Fiona.
Title: The STEM of airplanes / Fiona Young-Brown.
Description: Frst edition. | New York : Cavendish Square, 2021. | Series:The world of STEM | Includes index.
Identifiers: ISBN 9781502650047 (pbk.) | ISBN 9781502650061 (library bound) | ISBN 9781502650054 (6 pack) | ISBN 9781502650078 (ebook)
Subjects: LCSH: Airplanes–Juvenile literature. | Aeronautics–Juvenile literature. | Science–Juvenile literature. | Technology–Juvenile literature.
Classification: LCC TL547.Y68 2021 | DDC 629.133'34–dc23

Editor: Caitlyn Miller and Jennifer Lombardo
Copy Editor: Alex Tessman
Designer: Andrea Davison-Bartolotta

The photographs in this book are used by permission and through the courtesy of: Cover, p. 1 aapsky/Shutterstock.com; series art (texture) bestbrk/Shutterstock.com; p. 4 EmiliaUngur/Shutterstock.com; p. 6 Hulton Archive/Getty Images; p. 7 Universal History Archive/Universal Images Group via Getty Images; p. 8 Keystone-France/Gamma-Keystone via Getty Images; p. 10 Dawid Lech/Shutterstock.com; pp. 12–13 Alex Veresovich/Shutterstock.com; pp. 14–15 shaineast/Shutterstock.com; pp. 16–17 John Selway/Shutterstock.com; p. 18 Maciej Kopaniecki/Shutterstock.com; p. 20 Etaphop photo/Shutterstock.com; p. 22 Arterra/Universal Images Group via Getty Images; p. 23 Joe McNally/Getty Images; p. 24 Gene Blevins/AFP/Getty Images; p. 27 Flystock/Shutterstock.com; p. 28 MirasWonderland/Shutterstock.com; p. 29 Donald Iain Smith/Getty Images.

CPSIA compliance information: Batch #CS20CSQ: For further information contact Cavendish Square Publishing LLC, New York, New York, at 1-877-980-4450.

Printed in the United States of America

Contents

ASKING QUESTIONS AND SOLVING PROBLEMS

1

People have always dreamed of flying. The ancient Greeks told the story of Daedalus and Icarus. These two men used wings made of feathers and wax to fly. Icarus flew too close to the sun, and his wings melted. Today, technology helps people travel through the air, but people first had to solve many problems before they could fly.

THINK ON YOUR OWN

Why can birds fly but humans can't?

A fighter jet such as this one would have seemed like an impossible invention in the past.

Dreaming of Flight

Leonardo da Vinci drew detailed pictures of flying machines in the late 1400s and early 1500s. He studied the wings of bats and birds. Then, he drew a machine that worked the same way. This would allow a person to **glide** through the air. However, da Vinci never made any of these machines. Even if a person could have used the **mechanical** wings to fly, they would have needed a large amount of power to get off the ground.

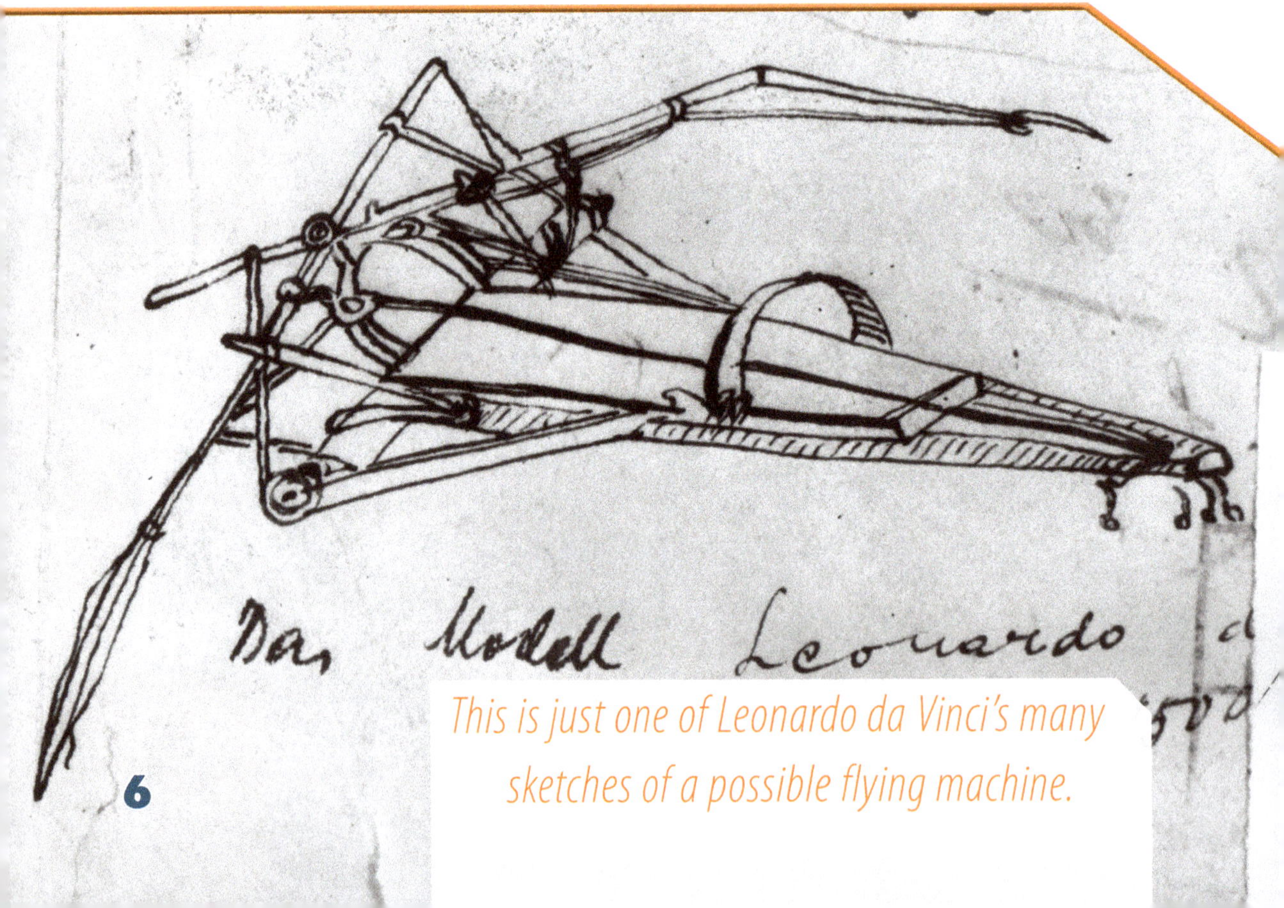

This is just one of Leonardo da Vinci's many sketches of a possible flying machine.

Nearly 300 years later, the first human flight took place. In 1783, the Montgolfier brothers flew in a hot air balloon in France. Balloons were not the best way to fly. They were hard to control. In windy weather, they were hard to steer, or drive. Balloons also needed a lot of gas for power, and that was dangerous, or unsafe. The gas could start a fire.

The first human flight happened in a hot air balloon similar to this one.

Taking to the Skies

A huge step forward in flight came in 1903. Near Kitty Hawk, North Carolina, the Wright brothers successfully

The first airplane was invented by brothers Orville and Wilbur Wright.

tested the first flying machine that looks like our airplanes today. An engine gave it enough power to get off the ground. Wings and **propellers** helped it fly. The first plane flew 120 feet (37 meters). The flight lasted 12 seconds.

After the Wright brothers made their flying machine, planes improved. People made faster, more powerful engines, bigger airplanes, and better **materials** to build them with. Thanks to jets, people can travel farther and more quickly than ever before. Fighter planes changed the way wars are fought. People can attack those they're fighting from the sky instead of sending soldiers into danger on land.

Today, engineers—people who build machines—face new challenges and seek new **solutions**. How can a plane travel farther? How can it carry more people or **cargo**? Can a fighter plane fly without being seen? Now, with **drones**, planes even fly without pilots. Engineers are shaping the future of flight every day!

THINK ON YOUR OWN

How have airplanes changed our everyday lives?

MATERIALS AND METHODS

2

Believe it or not, the Wright brothers' plane was made of wood, cloth, and wire. These materials were lightweight, cheap, and easy to find. However, they could also break easily; they weren't very strong. Wood can rot when it rains. As engines became more powerful and heavier, wood wasn't strong enough to build a plane that could fly higher safely.

THINK ON YOUR OWN

How does a heavy metal plane stay in the air?

Biplanes such as these were in use by the time World War I was fought.

Modern Materials

Today, we use many different materials to make airplanes. These include metals, such as steel, titanium, and aluminum. Sometimes, new **composite** materials, such as fiberglass or carbon fiber, are used. Steel is very strong and lasts a long time, but it's also heavy. This is why it's not used often for planes. Like steel,

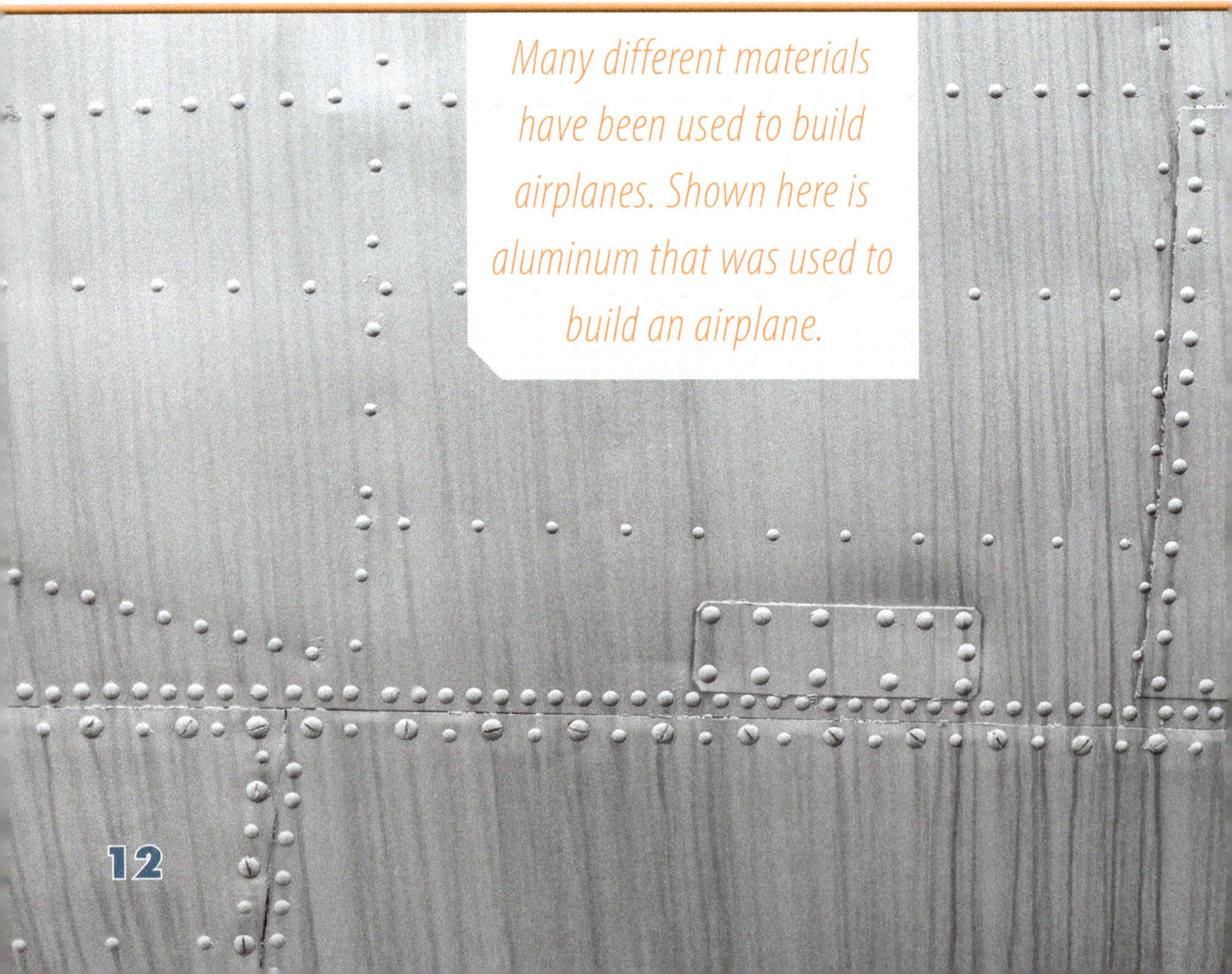

Many different materials have been used to build airplanes. Shown here is aluminum that was used to build an airplane.

titanium is also strong. It doesn't rust, and it's lighter than steel. It's sometimes used to build airplanes. Most planes are made from aluminum. Aluminum is strong and not expensive. More importantly, aluminum is very light.

Composite materials are even lighter than aluminum and can be stronger. They're used in some planes.

Some new passenger jets are made mostly from composite materials.

Weight Matters

It's important that a plane's materials are as light as possible. A lighter plane will be able to take off more easily. It will be easier to keep in the air too. A lighter airplane will also use less **fuel**. This means the cost of flying will be cheaper.

Engines

The first planes were powered by a simple engine. These engines were very small and not very powerful. Early planes couldn't fly far. Since then, engines have changed a lot. They've become much more powerful.

One challenge is to make new engines that are even more powerful but aren't too big. An engine that's too big or too heavy will need even more power to help the plane fly. The best engine would be powerful but also as small and light as possible.

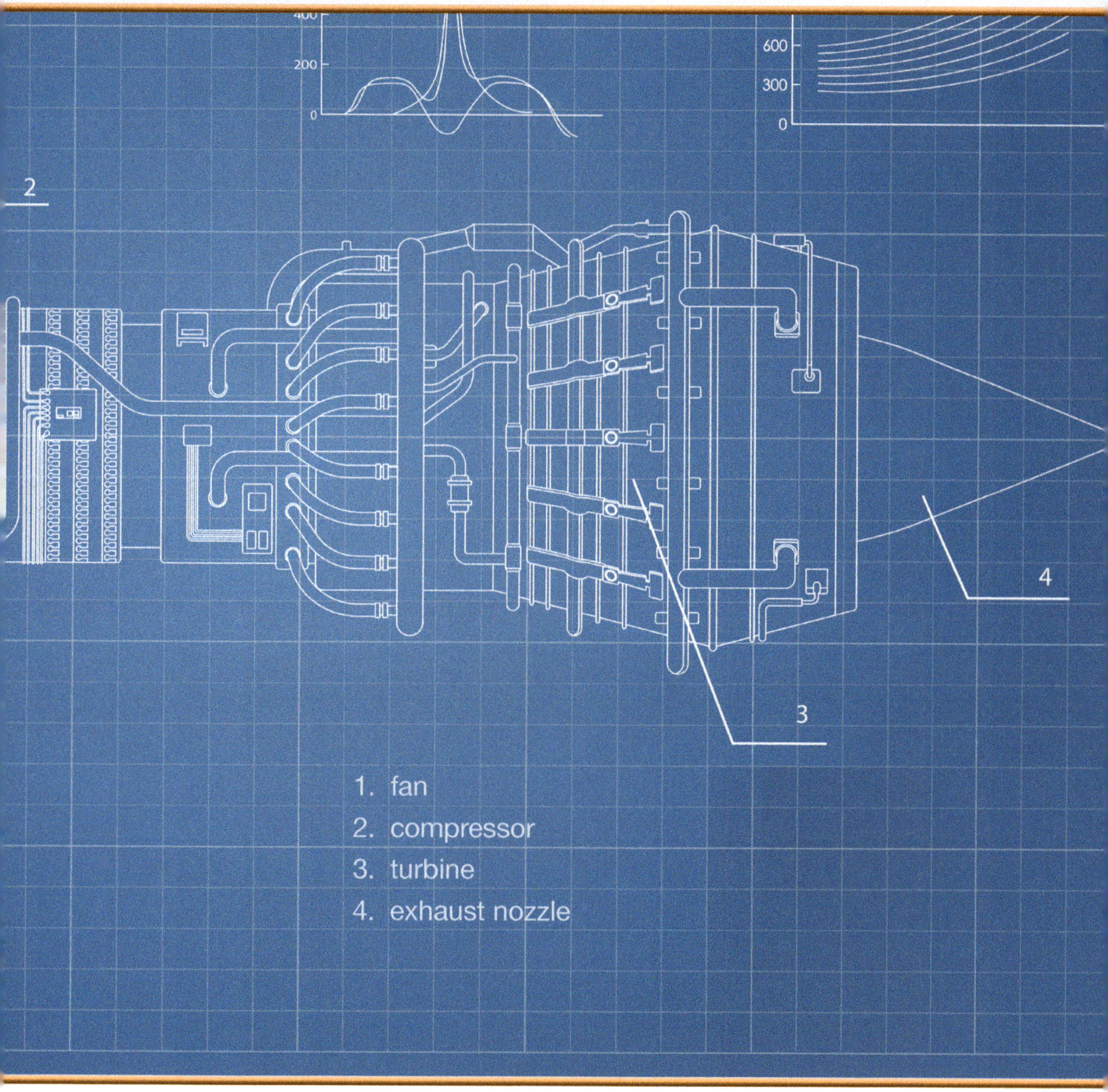

As this blueprint shows, modern jet engines have very complicated designs.

The Concorde was supersonic because it was so long, thin, and smooth.

Today's jet engines are extremely powerful. Some are even supersonic. "Supersonic" means that they can fly faster than the speed of sound. The Concorde was a famous supersonic plane. It could fly from London or Paris to New York City in about three hours!

THINK ON YOUR OWN

Why do bigger planes need a bigger engine or more engines?

4071

STEM IN ACTION

3

Different planes are used for different things. When engineers **design** a plane, they have to think about what its job is. A large plane, such as a Boeing 747, needs to carry a lot of people and cargo for a long distance. It will be very heavy. A smaller F-16 fighter plane needs to be very fast, but it doesn't carry as much weight. The planes need different designs to be able to do their jobs well. The shape of the wings, the body, and the nose of the plane all play a part in how fast a plane can go.

Fighter planes, such as this F-16, are designed for speed.

How Much Fuel?

Engineers need to calculate, or use math to find out, how much a plane will weigh with its pilot and any passengers or cargo. Then, they need to calculate how much fuel the plane will need to complete its journey. The fuel adds to the weight too, so this has to be included in their calculations.

Airplanes need fuel to get where they're going. A truck brings fuel to the plane.

When people go on a car trip, they usually make sure the fuel tank is full. Often, a plane will fly without a full fuel tank. This is because the weight of the fuel can slow the plane down. However, the calculations must be done correctly so there's enough fuel to fly!

THINK ON YOUR OWN

What are some ways to improve the gas mileage of an airplane?

Testing a Plane

To test a new plane design, engineers can use **computer simulations**. They can put things—including weight, speed, and wind conditions—into a computer. The simulation will calculate what will happen to the plane when different things change. For example, if more weight is added, will the plane fly?

A computer simulation can help pilots solve problems before they get in the air.

THINK ON YOUR OWN

How might we make an engine that's more powerful but smaller?

Another way to test a plane is to use a wind tunnel. This is a large tube with air inside. The air moves just like it would around a flying plane. A small model of the plane is put inside the tunnel first. Engineers can see how the plane will act in the sky. They can fix any problems before they build the real plane. Later, they might use a much bigger wind tunnel to test the full-size plane.

The way air moves around objects is called aerodynamics. Engineers use wind tunnels to test a plane's aerodynamics.

CUTTING-EDGE TECHNOLOGY

4

Can an airplane fly into space? That's one question engineers are asking. In 2018, the VSS *Unity* flew to the edges of space. The VSS *Unity* is not really an airplane, though. It's called a spaceplane because it's powered by rockets.

An airplane needs air to be able to fly. The engines push the air, which lets the plane fly. In space, there is no air. The VSS *Unity* uses rocket engines to push it forward, just like any other spacecraft. The force, or power, of the fuel burning is so strong that the *Unity* moves.

Engineers are still working to design an airplane that could fly into space. In the early

The VSS Unity *is a new type of plane called a spaceplane.*

1900s, the Wright brothers wanted to see if they could fly. Today, engineers are taking airplane technology to new heights! New kinds of airplanes are being designed all the time.

THINK ON YOUR OWN

How might it be possible to make a plane that can fly in both air and space?

A Plane Without a Pilot?

A drone is a kind of aircraft that doesn't have a person on board. It's controlled either by a person on the ground or by computers. Drones are lighter than most airplanes. This is because they don't carry any people. Drones are used for many different reasons. They can take pictures of an area. They can help find people who are lost. They're used to deliver medicines to people in some parts of the world.

Drones can be used for all sorts of jobs, including delivering the mail!

Engineers are testing new drone technologies. For example, one that uses **solar power** to fly might be able to stay in the air for months at a time. This would be useful for scientists collecting information, or facts, about weather or mapping areas that are hard to reach.

A Plane Made of Plants!

New composite materials are helping engineers design lighter aircraft. Carbon fiber is very light and strong.

One drawback is that it's expensive. New, stronger types of aluminum are being created. One new type of composite material is made from a plant called hemp. It's very strong and **environmentally friendly**. In 2015, a plane was made completely from hemp. Imagine flying in a plane made from plants!

Airplanes are always changing. Planes are being made from new materials. Some planes can fly themselves. Planes might one day go to space. Science, technology, engineering, and math are behind it all. Who knows what the future will bring?

One reason why hemp (shown here) is environmentally friendly is because, unlike trees, it grows back quickly after it's been cut.

What will planes look like in the future? This is one possible design.

THINK ON YOUR OWN

What do you think planes will be like in the future?

Glossary

cargo Something that is carried by an airplane.

composite Made by adding together two or more other materials together.

computer simulations A computer program that shows the way a machine might work.

design To create the plan for making something. Also, the way something has been made.

drone An aircraft that does not have a pilot but is controlled by computer or radio control.

environmentally friendly Good for the earth.

fuel A material such as coal, gas, or oil that is heated to provide power.

gas mileage The number of miles that can be traveled when a certain amount of fuel is used.

glide To fly without being powered by an engine.

material The substance used to build or create something.

mechanical Made or operated by machines.

propeller A spinning blade that is turned quickly by an engine and that helps an aircraft move.

solar power A type of power that changes energy from the sun into electricity.

solution An answer to a problem.

Find Out More

Books

Colby, Jennifer. *Birds to Aircraft*. North Mankato, MN: Cherry Lake Publishing, 2019.

DK. *The Big Book of Airplanes*. New York, NY: Dorling Kindersley, 2016.

Websites

How Things Fly

howthingsfly.si.edu

Hosted by the Smithsonian National Air and Space Museum, this website explains the science behind flight, including such topics as gravity, aerodynamics, and propulsion.

Up, Up, and Away! – Airplanes

teachengineering.org/curricularunits/view/cub_airplanes_curricularunit

Explore a series of lessons and activities related to how airplanes work, provided by the University of Colorado Boulder.

Publisher's note to educators and parents: Our editors have carefully reviewed these websites to ensure that they are suitable for students. Many websites change frequently, however, and we cannot guarantee that a site's future contents will continue to meet our high standards of quality and educational value. Be advised that students should be closely supervised whenever they access the Internet.

Index